Ethiopia
Travel Guide

Sightseeing, Hotel, Restaurant & Shopping Highlights

Christina Taylor

Table of Contents

Ethiopia

Ethiopia has no shortage of attractions and adventurous visitors can choose from hiking in the Simien Mountains to participating in watersports like angling and whitewater rafting. The country offers unique geographical features such as the Sof Omar Caves, the longest cave system in Africa.

Ethiopia is located in eastern Africa in the Horn of Africa and is surrounded by Sudan to the west, Kenya to the south, Somalia to the northeast and Djibouti and Eritrea to the north.

Ethiopia is an evocative land of contrasts. Its natural beauty ranges from the majestic Simien Mountains and the vast Blue Nile Falls, to the tranquillity of Lake Tana and the parched, salt-encrusted volcanic craters of the Danakil Depressions.

The country's population is also diverse. Northern Ethiopia's people descended from an ancient African civilization, and you will find some of the most remote and isolated tribal groupings in the Omo Valley in the southwestern part of the country.

The monasteries of Lake Tana and the cave churches of Lalibela and Tigray offer intriguing insights into religious traditions that go back to biblical times. In Axum, the enduring legend of the Queen of Sheba, a powerful African monarch who visited King Solomon, comes to life. It is here, allegedly, that the Arc of the Covenant, one of the holiest of Jewish relics, has resided for 3000 years.

Ethiopia's historical attractions provide rich glimpses into the world of medieval Africa, but Ethiopia's oldest relic is Lucy, a three million year old hominid that is arguably the world's most famous fossil. Pay homage to the country's proud and independent kings, by visiting the tomb of Menelik II and the cathedrals built by the former Emperor Haile Selassie. For a raw and tragic glimpse at the country's most recent history, include the Red Terror Museum in your itinerary.

Ethiopia has eleven national parks as well as a number of wildlife sanctuaries. It is home to a wild variety of animal life and over 900 bird species. Bring a pair of binoculars for a spot of bird watching.

Budget travellers will be pleasantly surprised by the affordable accommodations and eateries. Coffee lovers are in for a treat. In Ethiopia, the coffee ceremony is taken very seriously.

Culture

Ethiopia has an ancient culture that is influenced by Judaic traditions as well as old Greek texts. Its civilization arose from the Tigray, a Semitic speaking people, between 800 and 400 BC, and first found expression in the Aksumite Kingdom. The Tigray nobility are believed to be descended from Menelik I, the son of King Solomon and the Queen of Sheba.

The population of Ethiopia is made up of over 80 different ethnic groups and there are more than 90 different local languages. The most common language of these is Amharic, which represents about a quarter of the population and is also the official language. Other languages include Afaan Oromo, Tigrinya and Somali. English is the most widely spoken foreign language. Arabic is also taught.

The rich diversity of Ethiopia's culture incorporates various elements including song and dance, incorporating a variety of traditional instruments. Around 43 percent of the country's inhabitants belong to the Ethiopian Orthodox Church with a smaller group of 33 percent being Muslim and roughly 18 percent professing an affiliation to various Protestant churches. In general you will find the greatest concentration of Muslims in the low-lying parts of Ethiopia to the south and east of the country, while the majority of Christians live in the more elevated regions.

The country has many delightful customs. The coffee ceremony is a stylish affair that involves the strewing of flowers and the burning of incense. Another custom is the observance of fasting days, according to the calendar of the Ethiopian Orthodox Church. Fasting is observed on Wednesday's and Friday's as well as during religious periods such as prior to Orthodox Easter. When fasting, one daily meal is taken and this should have no meat, eggs, fat or dairy products.

The country is religious and fairly conservative, with gender roles being clearly defined. Dress respectfully when visiting religious sites. Visitors should bear in mind that some of the religious sites, such as monasteries, do not allow women. At religious buildings that do allow women, it is often requested that females cover their heads and shoulders with scarves. The word 'faranji' or 'fereng' is sometimes used to refer to Europeans.

Location & Orientation

The country is divided into nine regions that were determined by their ethnic makeup. These are Afar, Tigray, Amhara, Oromia, Benishangul-Gumuz, Gambela, Harari, Somali and the South Nations, Nationalities and Peoples Region.

Ethiopia is mountainous and a section of the Great Rift Valley, the Eastern Rift passes through the country.

The capital of Ethiopia is Addis Ababa and its airport, Bole International, is one of the busiest airports in East Africa, with connecting flights to Djibouti, Dar es Salaam, Cairo, Nairobi, Dakar, Brazzaville, Harare and Johannesburg. There are daily flights from several international airlines connecting Ethiopia to various cities in Europe, Asia and the USA. Internal flights connect the capital to various centers such as Bahir Dar, Gondar, Lalibela and Axum.

One of the great challenges of a sightseeing holiday in Ethiopia is the distances that need to be covered. Although there is a network of bus routes that covers the country at fairly economical rates, this is a slow form of travel, as there is usually only one bus per day. You will be charged extra for luggage. The main bus terminal in Addis Ababa is Autobus Terra.

For inner city travel, minibuses are cheap and quick. Another budget way of getting around a town or city is by bajaj (the bajaj is a three-wheeled vehicle which the locals refer to as a taxi) and can cost as little as 1 to 2 birr per person. In the southern part of the country, the terrain can be hazardous, and it is best to travel in a 4x4 vehicle. If you are considering renting your own car, think again as Ethiopia does not recognize International Driving Permits.

Climate & When to Visit

Ethiopia is located within the tropical zone between the Equator and the Tropic of Cancer and its climate is largely determined by its elevation above sea level. Temperatures are roughly the same year round, and there is a wet or monsoon season that occurs between June and September. The country can be divided into three distinct climate zones.

The Tropical Zone (known locally as Kolla) experiences hot and humid weather and can be found at elevations of 1830m and under. The annual average is about 27 degrees Celsius, but this zone includes areas such as the Danakil Depression, where temperatures can rise as high as 50 degrees Celsius. The Subtropical Zone (also called Woina Dega) can be found at an altitude of between 1830 and 2440m and this includes towns and cities such as Addis Ababa, Mekele, Axum, Gondar and Bahar Dar. For example, Addis Ababa sees day temperatures between 20 and 24 degrees Celsius and night temperatures between 7 and 11 degrees Celsius.

Occasionally, temperatures in the capital can fall as low as 4 degrees Celsius. Bahar Dar is somewhat warmer with day temperatures between 23 and 30 degrees Celsius and night temperatures of 10 to 16 degrees Celsius. In Gondar, you can expect day temperatures between 21 and 29 degrees Celsius and night averages from 12 to 17 degrees Celsius. The Cool Zone (locally referred to as Dega) occurs at elevations above 2440m and includes places such as Lalibela. Here, temperature averages of around 16 degrees Celsius can be expected and annual rainfall figures are recorded at between 1270 and 1280mm.

Generally the period between April and May tends to be the hottest in most parts of the country, while August is usually the coolest. Most of the country's rainfall occurs between June and September, with heaviest precipitation being experienced during July and August.

Sightseeing Highlights

Addis Ababa

In Amharic, Addis Ababa means "New Flower" and at an altitude of 2400m, it is the third highest capital in the world. A great way to experience the "lay of the land" and enjoy the spectacular scenery is by taking a trip to the summit of Entoto Hill, which towers over the capital at an elevation of 3,200m. The peak is covered with eucalyptus trees imported from Australia during the time of King Menelik II. It is also the site of his old palace and the Maryam Church.

An important stop for many visitors to Addis Ababa is the National Museum of Ethiopia and its star exhibit is Lucy, a three million year old hominid fossil. She was discovered in 1974 by Donald Johanson, an American paleoanthropologist in Hadar and is known locally as "dinkness" or the wondrous one.

Other displays include early pottery, carvings and artwork, as well as the throne of Emperor Haile Selassie I. For a harrowing look at Ethiopia's more recent history, stop off at the Red Terror Martyrs Memorial Museum on Bole Street just off the Meksele Square which is also known as Revolutionary Square. Well-curated and informative, the Red Terror Martyrs Museum documents the horror of the bloody regime of Haile Mengistu Maryam using photographs, artwork and other material. It includes an ossuary displaying the mortal remains of many of the period's political victims. Admission is free, but donations are welcome.

Addis Ababa was founded in 1887 by King Menelik II who history remembers as one of the great unifiers and modernisers of Ethiopia. During his reign, Menelik II introduced the country to telephones and electricity, built schools and hospitals, envisaged the laying of a railway from Addis Ababa to Djibouti and successfully repelled attempts by Italy to subject the country to colonial rule.

Visitors can pay homage to this visionary leader of Africa by visiting the grand mausoleum constructed in his honor by his daughter, Empress Zawditu. The shrine is located near the Kidane Mihret church and incorporates motifs of lions, as well as the star of David to emphasize the legendary connection between the Ethiopian emperors and the biblical King Solomon.

There are murals inside depicting scenes from the life of Menelik II and the remains of other members of the royal family such as Empress Taitu and Empress Zawditu are also buried here. At the Holy Trinity Cathedral, you can visit the tomb of Haile Selassie I and the grave of the British suffragette, Sylvia Pankhurst who died in Addis Ababa.

Lalibela

The dusty town of Lalibela was named after a devout Ethiopian king of the 12th century and the legacy of his awe-inspiring cave churches remains an enigma. Lalibela was shown the great churches of Jerusalem while in exile and when he learnt later that Muslims had captured the Holy City in 1187, he declared that the town of Roha should become a New Jerusalem. A series of monolithic churches were hewn from red volcanic rock and today, archaeologists remain baffled by the grand scale of the complex, as well as the methods by which the churches might have been constructed. Legends suggest divine intervention and angelic labor and experts remain at odds to disprove this bold claim.

The most striking of the churches is the Church of St George or Bet Giyorgis. This was allegedly inspired by a vision of St George and its roof features the relief work of three Greek crosses, set inside each other. The church is shaped like a cross and its location, inside a deep pit means that it can only be accessed via a tunnel. Another popular church is Bet Maryam, the Church of St Mary, where visitors can admire a series of beautiful frescoes. An interesting painting focusses on two women, sitting side by side with their babes. They are the Queen of Sheba and her handmaiden. According to legend, the handmaiden also bore King Solomon a son and he founded the Zagwa dynasty as well as the original settlement at Lalibela. Bet Medhame Alem is notable for its enormous dimensions. It is considered the largest rock hewn church in the world.

Be prepared to spend at least a day, or possibly two days exploring all the churches. Admission is $50 and will give visitors a four-day pass to the area of the churches, but to get the most out of a trip, you should consider recruiting a local guide. You will also be expected to tip the guardians at the door of each of the churches you visit. It is required that visitors remove their shoes when entering a church and ladies are expected to cover up with a shawl or scarf. Visitors with reduced mobility may find the uneven terrain and steep paths challenging.

Bahar Dar

Bahar Dar, also called Bahir Dar, is the capital of the Amhara region. It is located on the Northern Plateau along the southern shores of Lake Tana at an altitude of about 1,800m above sea level and dates back to the 16th or 17th century.

As the largest body of water in Ethiopia and the source of the Blue Nile, Lake Tana is one of the main attractions of Bahar Dar. The timeless papyrus tankwa boats used by traditional fishermen in the region will remind visitors of ancient Egypt and in its brown, silty waters you can expect to encounter the odd hippo or crocodile, as well as an abundance of bird life such as pelicans and fish eagles.

The highlight of a boat trip on the lake is a visit to the island monasteries, which were founded between the 13th and 17th centuries. Particularly interesting is the monastery at Ura Kidane Meret on the Zege Peninsula. Here you will be able to see a beautiful collection of murals and other artwork, including the crowns of several past emperors. The monastery was founded during the 14th century by Saint Betre Mariyam and is widely regarded as one of the most beautiful of the island monasteries. Other monasteries worth a visit include Daga Istafanos, which has a 15th century painting of the Madonna and includes a mausoleum with the remains of five Ethiopian emperors and Tana Chirkos, which allegedly held the Ark of the Covenant for several centuries. Do bear in mind that some of the monasteries limit admission to men only and can only be visited by special arrangement.

Bahar Dar also offers access to the Blue Nile Falls, which is Africa's second largest waterfall, after the Victoria Falls. Also known as Tis Issat or "smoking water", the falls extend over 400m and have a drop of between 37 and 45m. In the rainy season, there are four distinct streams and the surrounding area features many plant and animal species found only in this part of Africa.

Nearby, you can also see the Portuguese Bridge, one of the oldest bridges in Ethiopia. The bulk of water from the Blue Nile Falls is now diverted to power a hydro-electric plant, but if you schedule your visit for a Sunday or public holiday when this facility is closed, you will still be able to view the waterfall in all its spectacular glory. It is at its most impressive during the rainy season, which lasts from July to September. The Blue Nile Falls is located about 30km downstream from Bahar Dar.

Gondar

Located just north of Lake Tana, Gondar became the capital for the nomadic Solomanic Emperors and served in that role for around 200 years. It was also once home to the falashas, a Jewish splinter group, who had been isolated from mainstream Judaism since 650BC, although most of these were evacuated to Israel during the 1980s and early 1990s.

The city's main attraction is Fasil Ghebbi, a medieval compound of 70,000 square meters sometimes referred to as Africa's Camelot. There are several castles within the complex, of which the most significant is no doubt that of Emperor Fasilados. The baths are likewise associated with his era and are still used for baptisms.

The palace of Iyasu I is the largest of the group and other structures include stables, a banqueting hall, a library and three churches. Make sure you pay a visit to the Debre Berhan Selassie Church. It was built in the 17th century by Emperor Eyasu II and was one of few churches to survive an attack on Gondar by the Mahdist Dervishes of the Sudan in 1888.

Divine intervention came in the form of a swarm of bees that prevented access to the invaders. Its biblical murals are of exceptional quality. The structures, which have been restored, show elements of Ethiopian and Baroque architecture. Fasil Ghebbi has been declared a UNESCO World Heritage Site.

While in the neighborhood, consider a day trip to the nearby town of Gongora. Its 17th century church, the Church of Debre Sina has an interesting collection of Biblical paintings and some of the northern Lake Tana monasteries are equally accessible from here.

Simien Mountains National Park

The dramatic landscape of jagged peaks and deep valleys that characterizes the Simien Mountains National Park was created by erosion over millions of years. It is home to a number of rare endemic wildlife of Northern Ethiopia, such as the Walia ibex, the Simien or Ethiopian wolf and the Gelada baboon. Other species include the Anubis Baboon, the Hamadryas baboon, the klipspringer and the golden jackal. There are also over 130 bird species, of which 16 are endemic to the Ethiopia/Eritrea area. An important presence is its colony of lammergeyer vultures.

The Simien Mountains are of basalt rock and volcanic in origin, but in winter, they are covered with snow. It is here that you will find the highest mountain in Ethiopia, a cluster of nine peaks known as Ras Dashen that reaches the impressive height of 4,550m. The ruin of a fort at 4,300m serves as a reminder that this was the scene of a 19th century battle. The mountains are rumored to be inhabited by malevolent spirits.

Axum

There are several legends associated with the city of Axum. It is believed to have been home to the Queen of Sheba and there are also claims that the biblical Ark of the Covenant resides in one of its churches. According to history, it was the original capital of the ancient Kingdom of Aksum, which minted its own coins and thrived by facilitating trade with Rome and India.

The most visible reminders of the city's illustrious past are the Stelae, a series of stone towers or obelisks believed to be around 1,700 years old. One of the most striking of these is the Obelisk of Axum, which stands 24m tall and weighs around 160 tons. The granite structure is decorated with several false doors and windows. After being removed by the Italians, it was displayed in Rome for several decades until its return to Ethiopia around 2008. A collection of stelae can be viewed at Northern Stelae Park. The centerpiece is King Ezana's Stela, one of the smaller ones at 21m. Another striking example is the 33m Great Stela, which lies broken. There are a number of lesser stela of between 18 and 15m. A 20 minutes walk from the site, you can visit the tombs of kings Kaleb and Gebre Meskel. Near the quarry where stone for the stelae was mined, you may find the Lioness of Gobedra.

Another archaeological treasure of Axum is the Ezana stone. The text of the stone chronicles a battle in which King Ezana defeated six other kings, but what makes it interesting is the fact that the details are inscribed in three different languages - Sabaean, an old form of south Arabic spoken in Yemen, Ge'ez, which was the official language used in the Kingdom of Aksum and Greek. As such, it provides a linguistic key similar to the Rosetta Stone.

There are two important churches, both dedicated to St Mary of Zion, in Axum. They can be found beside each other. The Old Cathedral was built in 1665 by the Emperor Fasilides on the site of several prior places of worship. The original was believed to have been built by Ezana after his conversion to Christianity.

The New Cathedral was constructed by Haile Selassie to fulfil a pledge and has beautiful stained glass windows and paintings. A third building, the Chapel of the Tablet, is believed to house the Ark of the Covenant, but it is not open to the public. This is believed to be the holiest site in Ethiopia.

Other attractions of Axum include a ruin widely regarded as the Palace of the Queen of Sheba (although it is dated from the 7th century AD), the Monastery of Abba Pantaleon, which unfortunately admits only male visitors and the Archaeological Museum, which has a number of stone artefacts. Axum is located in the Tigray region, at an altitude of 2,131m.

Oromia Region & Sof Omar Caves

The Oromia Region is home to the Oromo tribe and has smaller groups of the Amhara and Gurage peoples. For nature lovers it offers several unique landscapes and the chance to view some of its rarest animal species up close, but do bear in mind that many of its attractions are best accessible via four wheel drive vehicles, due to the poor conditions of some of the roads.

Visit the Bala Mountains National Park for a rare look at some flora and fauna endemic to Ethiopia, but found virtually nowhere else. The largest concentrations of the severely endangered Ethiopian wolf and the mountain nyala reside here.

Other wildlife includes Menelik's bushbuck, the warthog and the bohor reedbuck. On the Sanetti Plateau you can see examples of the unique giant lobelia, a plant species found only at altitudes above 3,100m and, if you are up to a spot of mountaineering, consider tackling Tullu Dimtu, at 4,389m the second highest peak in Ethiopia or Mount Batu, at a slightly more modest 4,307m. In the southern part of the park lies the Harenna Forest, home to many of Ethiopia's endemic animal and bird species. The Bale Mountains National Park can be found south of the Awash River.

There are several trails in the beautiful surroundings of Wenchi Crater Lake, ranging from the 4km Fincha trail that rounds the rim of the crater to the 16km Bagoba-Abagalalcha trail, which takes you down into the valley to the Dawala hot springs and waterfall. Take good walking shoes and bear in mind that you might get your feet wet. Horseback riding is another option for exploring this peaceful location. A boat trip to an island monastery and Kirkos church can also be included. The area is home to a diverse collection of wildlife and terrestrial as well as aquatic birds. An excursion costs US$12 or 100 birr per day, excluding refreshments.

One of the most spectacular natural structures of the Oromiya Region is the Sof Omar Caves, which is at 15.1km, the longest network of caves in Africa. The caves are formed by the underground passage of the Weib river and include many interesting features, such as the Chamber of Columns and over 40 entry or exit points, although only about four of these remain functional. The cave is named after Sheik Sof Omar Ahmed, a Muslim saint who sheltered here during the 11th century. It is now considered a Muslim shrine. The main entrance for visitors is from a narrow footpath behind a cliff top village, also named Sof Omar, which is located above the Weib river. The cave system has been declared a UNESCO World Heritage Site. The Sof Omar caves lie 120km east of the city of Robe.

Other attractions in the Oromiya region include Lake Shala, which is at a depth of 266m, the deepest of the Rift Valley lakes. Lake Shala is home to colonies of flamingo to the south and pelicans on its various islands. The lake has various hot springs, which causes its distinctively foggy atmosphere.

Omo Valley

The Omo Valley is located in the southwestern part of Ethiopia. The region is home to eight different tribes and around 200,000 indigenous people, but is also known for its relatively unspoilt biodiversity. There are more than 80 large mammal species and around 300 bird species. Some of its wildlife includes leopards, lions, cheetahs, elephants, giraffes, buffaloes, rhinos, gazelles, zebras, hippos, kudus, eland and various types of monkeys such as the Blue Monkey, Patas Monkey and Colobus Monkey. Its rivers are inhabited by the Nile Crocodile, Africa's largest crocodile species.

Two national parks can be found in the valley. These are the Omo National Park and the Mago National Park. The Mago National Park includes Mount Mago and the Tama Wildlife Reserve and its grasslands are home to a rich variety of animal life. The Omo National Park is the largest of the two and besides the wildlife, it offers access to a number of colorful tribes such as the Suri, the Dizi, the Me'en and the Mursi. The cultural experience of tribal life is what draws most visitors to the Omo Valley.

One tribal group most people find memorable and fascinating is the Mursi. Women of the tribe still wear lip plates of clay. This striking form of body modification involves the piercing of the lower lip, after which it is stretched through the addition of first wooden plugs and then clay lip plates that are gradually increased in size. Some sources suggest that the size of a woman's lip plate is related to the value of her dowry, but this is unconfirmed. The custom is connected with a girl's passage to womanhood and also with perceptions of a family's status and prosperity. Until recently, the Mursi were among the most isolated peoples.

Other customs and rituals on display include scarification, dances and demonstrations of tribal crafts and chores, such as preparing food and separating grain. Among the Hamar, you might witness a rite known as bull jumping which is practiced as a test of manhood. Some of the villages to include in the itinerary include Jinka, the region's capital, Konso, Turmi, Karo, Dimeka and Chencha. The towns of Jinka and Arba Minch, which is the last large town before you reach the Omo Valley are accessible by air and can be used as a starting point for an excursion, which will typically take between 8 and 14 days. Various packages are also available.

http://www.wildfrontierstravel.com/en_GB/destination/ethiopia/group-tours/master/2000303/ethiopia-tribes-of-the-omo-valley-1
http://www.exploreethiopiatours.com/Cultural-tour-Omo-Valley-Ethiopia.html

Harar

The walled city of Harar has been a commercial junction that linked trade routes from the Arabian Peninsula to the Horn of Africa for several centuries. It is considered the 4th holiest Muslim city and entry was once forbidden to all infidels. Most of its inhabitants are Muslim and the city has 82 mosques and 102 shrines. It also provides easy access to the Awash National Park and the Babile Elephant Sanctuary. At Harar, you can witness the nocturnal feeding of the city's population of spotted hyena. According to folklore, the hyenas have co-existed with the people of the city for 500 years.

Danakil Depression

One of the more unusual landscapes of Ethiopia is the Danakil Depression, which can be found in Afar, near the border with Eritrea and Djibouti. It is one of the hottest and most forbidding places on earth. It is here that the Awash River dries up into a series of scattered salt lakes. Some of the unusual features include Lake Asele, at 90m below sea level, one of the lowest places on earth and the multi-colored salt deposits around Dallol Mountain, caused by volcanic action below the salt. Another volcano, Erta Ale, is so active that it includes a rare attribute - an active lava lake.

Recommendations for the Budget Traveller

Places to Stay

Afro Land Lodge

Gabon Road, Bole
Addis Ababa, Ethiopia
Tel: +251 (0)11 466 9228
http://www.afrolandlodge.com/

The Afro Land Lodge offers visitors to Addis Ababa the convenience of a central location and a modern establishment with reliable electricity and credit card facilities.

There are twelve spacious guest suites and all include a private bathroom, kitchenette with a microwave, fridge and kettle, a mini bar, satellite TV and free high-speed internet. There is also a free shuttle service. Accommodation begins at 875 birr ($43) and includes breakfast.

Red Rock Lalibela Hotel

Lalibela, Ethiopia
Tel: +251 (0)33 336 1030
http://www.redrocklalibelahotel.com/

The Red Rock Lalibela Hotel is a small, relatively modern hotel, which offers guests a quiet location that is within walking distance of the cave churches as well as the city center. There is a restaurant where guests can enjoy a complimentary coffee ceremony and guides can be arranged through the hotel. Some of the rooms offer great valley and mountain views, as well as the opportunity to indulge in a spot of bird watching. Rooms are basic, but clean and offer private bathrooms with hot water, as well as the convenience of free Wi-Fi coverage.
Accommodation begins at 462 birr ($23) with breakfast.

Homland Hotel

Main Airport Road, Bahar Dar, Ethiopia
Tel: +251 582 22 02 20
http://homlandhotelbahirdar.com/

Although Homland Hotel is located a little further from the lake than some of the older hotels, it does offer guests spacious and beautifully furnished rooms and friendly service. There is a free airport shuttle service, as well as a restaurant, free parking and 24 hour reception.

Rooms include satellite TV, with international channels such as CNN and the BBC, a fridge, mini bar, shower and free high-speed internet. Accommodation begins at 685 birr ($34) and includes breakfast. Half board and full board rates are also available.

Kereyu Hill Resort

Adama, Nazret, Ethiopia
Tel: +251-(0) 22 122 70 8
http://kereyuhillresorthotel.com/

As a small hotel located in Adama, the Kereyu Hill Resort offers a tranquil atmosphere and panoramic views that include the Rift Valley combined with a luxurious and affordable stay. The hotel has a restaurant that serves traditional and international cuisine. There is a swimming pool, sauna and children's play area. Free parking and a shuttle service is also available and some of the activities that can be enjoyed in the area include hiking and bird-watching. The service is excellent and friendly. Rooms are spacious, clean and meticulously maintained with satellite TV, a mini bar, fridge and free Wi-Fi coverage. Accommodation begins at 522 birr ($26) and includes a buffet breakfast.

Atse Kaleb Hotel

Ezama Square,
Axum, Ethiopia
Tel: +34 775 2222

The tranquil terrace and garden at the Atse Kaleb Hotel can be a real treat for bird lovers, as it attracts around 22 different bird species and staff may offer to help you spot and identify these avian visitors with the hotel's guide book.

The hotel is also located near a number of Axum's attractions, including the cathedral complex. There is an on-site restaurant and bar/lounge as well as a business center, a shuttle service and free parking. Rooms include a safe deposit box, hot shower facilities and free high-speed internet. Accommodation begins at 601 birr ($30) and includes breakfast.

Places to Eat

Yod Abyssinia

Bole Medhaniyalem Area,
Addis Ababa Ethiopia
Tel: 01-661-2985
http://www.yodethiopia.com

Prepare to experience a rich slice of Ethiopian culture, when you venture through the doors at Yod Abyssinia. Besides the food, you will be treated to a mesmerizing performance of traditional dancing accompanied by ethnic music. Audience participation is encouraged at certain points of the show.

The ambiance of the place is also enhanced by the authentic decor and the restaurant enjoys wide support from locals. There is a great mix of meat and vegetarian options and you can choose from dishes such as the spicy goat kofte, doro wat and kifto. Both light and dark injera bread is served and a popular budget option is the generous fasting platter, where you can choose from a number of vegetarian options for only 200 birr ($10). For beverages, try the Tej, a local honey wine served in pot-bellied jars.

Gusto Restaurant

3rd Floor, Tracon Tower
(In front of the Black Lion High School),
Addis Ababa, Ethiopia
Tel: +251 93 449 7861
http://www.gustorestaurante.com

It is perhaps thanks to the brief period of Italian rule, that
Ethiopia still has a fair amount of Italian restaurants. One of the
best is Gusto Restaurant, which is centrally located opposite the
French Lycee. There is live entertainment and diners have the
option of enjoying an outdoor veranda, with views of the city.
The atmosphere is relaxing. The salad bar, which offers a wide
selection of vegetable choices, can serve as appetizer and some
of the main dishes include pasta choices such as gnocchi,
risotto, pizza and osso bucco, also known as the rib-eyed steak.
There are even a few seafood choices like the grouper with
orange sauce, the penne with octopus or the salmon linguine,
but these are infrequently available. Gusto Restaurant also
offers diners a great selection of wines.

Ben Abeba Restaurant

Sekota Road, Lalibela, Ethiopia
http://www.benabeba.com

The architecture of the Ben Abeba Restaurant, sometimes
referred to as "the space ship" by locals, is reminiscent of the art
of Dali and Gaudi, incorporating interesting curves, winding
paths and eclectic viewing platforms. It seems designed to make
the most of the area's stunning valley and surrounding mountain
views.

The scenery can be particularly breathtaking at sunset. The menu features a combination of Scottish, Ethiopian and international cuisine made from fresh, organic ingredients and includes burgers, lentil soup, fish cakes, injera and smoothies. Favorites are the shepherd's pie and a dish known as 'bubble and squeak'. Service is accommodating and friendly. Expect to pay less than 325 birr ($16) per person for a three-course meal plus drinks.

Lake Shore Restaurant

Bahar Dar, Ethiopia

The best place to dine in Bahir Dar is right by Lake Tana and the Lake Shore restaurant, which is located on a hillside, offers visitors spectacular views of the lake and some of its avian inhabitants such as kingfishers, cormorants and pelicans. The atmosphere is relaxing and the serving staff are very friendly. The house speciality is tilapia (a freshwater fish species indigenous to Lake Tana) baked in foil in vegetables. It is served rather dramatically while still on fire. Other dishes available include injera, lentil soup, roasted chicken and burgers. Portions are extremely generous.

Habesha Kitfo

Gondar, Ethiopia

At Habesha Kitfo you can enjoy an authentic interior, complete with cowhide chairs and rugs woven from wool as well as live entertainment in the form of azmaris or Ethiopian folk singers. There is also an art gallery downstairs, when you can buy souvenirs.

The house speciality is kitfo, which can be ordered with lamb or minced beef and another favorite is lamb key wat, served with injera hard-boiled eggs. A full vegetarian fasting platter is available on a daily basis. Main dishes are priced at between 30 and 65 birr ($1.50 and $3.25).

Places to Shop

Sabahar

Mekannisa (behind the Salem Nurses College)
Addis Ababa, Ethiopia
Tel: +251 11 321 5221
http://sabahar.com/

Sabahar produced silk and other textiles handmade in Ethiopia and strives to adhere to fair trade standards for all of its workers, by paying fair wages and providing good and healthy working conditions. Founded in 2001, the organization now employs over 50 permanent workers as well as 70 home crafters, who do spinning and weaving.

Natural dyes from local plants and herbs are used to create vivid designs. The beautiful range includes hand and bath towels, scarves and shawls, cushions, throws and table linen. Wares are exported internationally, but Sabahar also have a shop in Addis Ababa, where you can view the various stages of the process - from cocoon, to finished article.

Buying Coffee in Addis Ababa

The Coffee Arabica plant originated in Ethiopia and today coffee is one of the country's most important crops. Most of its cultivation is for the export market, but there are a number of shops where you can buy Ethiopian coffee beans to take home.

There are two main types of coffee beans you should look out for. Harar beans are grown in the Eastern highlands and known of a rich full-bodied taste that is fruity, yet reminiscent of mocha. Sidamo beans are grown in the Sidamo Province and have a floral, spicy aroma with just a hint of citrus.

One of the best coffee shops to visit is Alem Bunna, where you will find a licensed coffee taster and a master roaster. Blends are sold in different sizes ranging from 25g to 1kg and larger bulk orders can be made up on request. Alem Bunna (http://www.alembunna.com/) has outlets in Addis Ababa along the Airport Road and on Bole Avenue, opposite the Angolan Embassy.

The Tomoca coffee shop (http://www.tomocacoffee.com/) may look quaint and somewhat antique, but it has been in business since 1953 and has established a well-earned reputation for one of the best brews in Ethiopia. Mokarar Coffee Shop, also known locally as Harar Coffee shop, is a favorite with the people of Addis Ababa. Soak up the friendly atmosphere and the aroma of coffee roasting in a wood-fired oven. Mokarar is located on Dejazmach Belay Zeleke Street and also sells top quality roasted beans.

Merkato

Addis Ababa, Ethiopia

There is no definite beginning or end point to the Merkato. It claims to be the largest open-air market in Africa and to get an idea of its dimensions, consider the following statistics. The sprawling market creates work for around 13,000 individuals and represents over 7000 separate business entities. Located in the Addis Ketema district, it is near the Al-Anwar Mosque.

The layout is a rather chaotic, but you will encounter local traders and crafters, some of whom still use pack donkeys to transport their goods. There are also many onsite tailors plying their trade. Some of the goods you can expect include shoes, traditional Ethiopian garments, bed covers, textiles and fabrics, spices and herbs, carved masks, silverware, wood crafted items, handbags, leather goods, shawls, souvenirs and religious relics.

You can buy coffee beans and the traditional jebena or clay pots used to brew it. Prepare yourself for some fierce haggling, though and do keep an eye on your possessions, as there are pickpockets about.

Salem's Ethiopia

Bole, Addis Ababa, Ethiopia
Tel: +251 (0) 911 645 619
http://www.salemsethiopia.com/

Salem's Ethiopia combines the crafts of basket-weaving, beading, cotton spinning and more to offer tourists a multi-layered cultural shopping experience. The basketry section has a range of beautiful crafted products, in different sizes and incorporating a variety of colorful designs.

You can choose from a selection of beautiful scarves to accessorize or buy some souvenirs for the home, in the form of napkins, placemats, rugs, throws and tablecloths. Jewellery includes pendants, necklaces, bracelets, rings and earrings. A variety of beads and gems are combined with silver.

Haileselassie Alemayehu

Churchill Ave,
Addis Ababa, Ethiopia

If you are tired of the relentless haggling that takes place in the markets, make your way to Haileselassie Alemayehu. The prices are fixed but generally fair. You can choose from a large selection of silver jewellery and and there is also a bead section that lets you mix and match your own combinations. Other items include woodcarvings, icons, baskets, paintings and traditional clothing.

CPSIA information can be obtained
at www.ICGtesting.com
Printed in the USA
LVOW01s1503281015

460124LV00016B/844/P